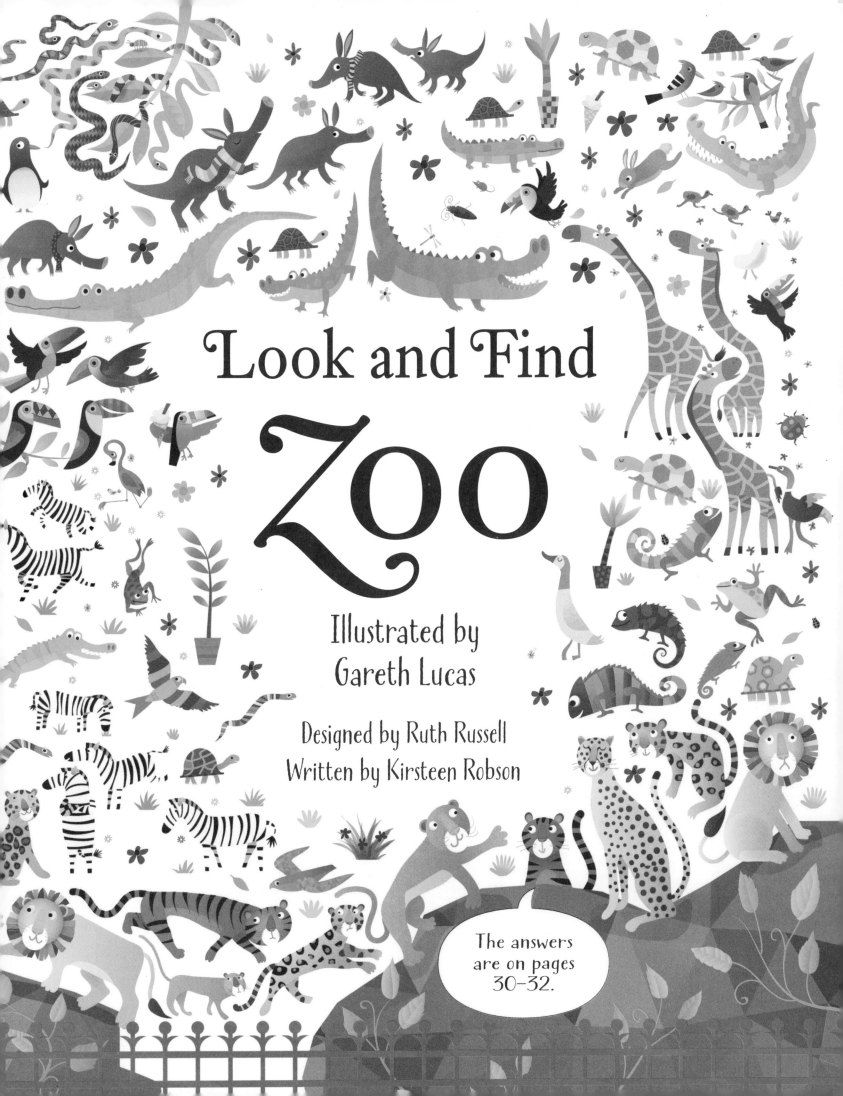

Look and Find

Zoo

Illustrated by
Gareth Lucas

Designed by Ruth Russell
Written by Kirsteen Robson

The answers
are on pages
30–32.

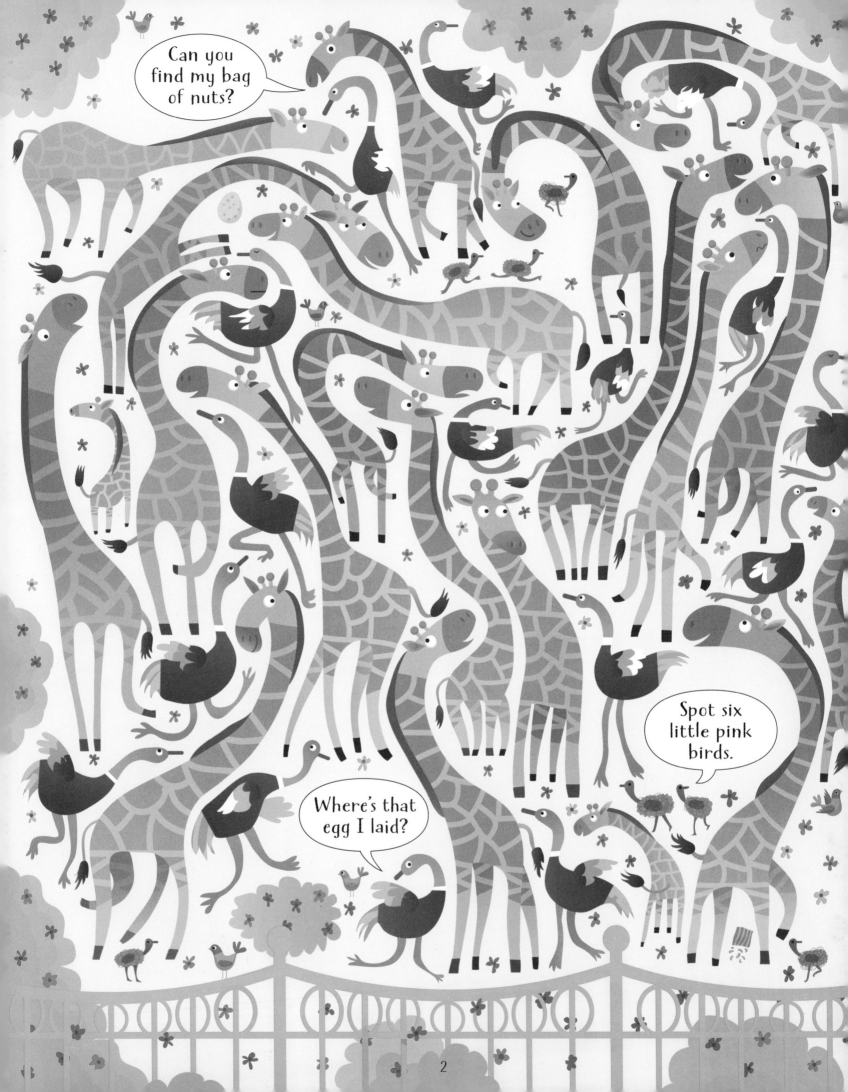

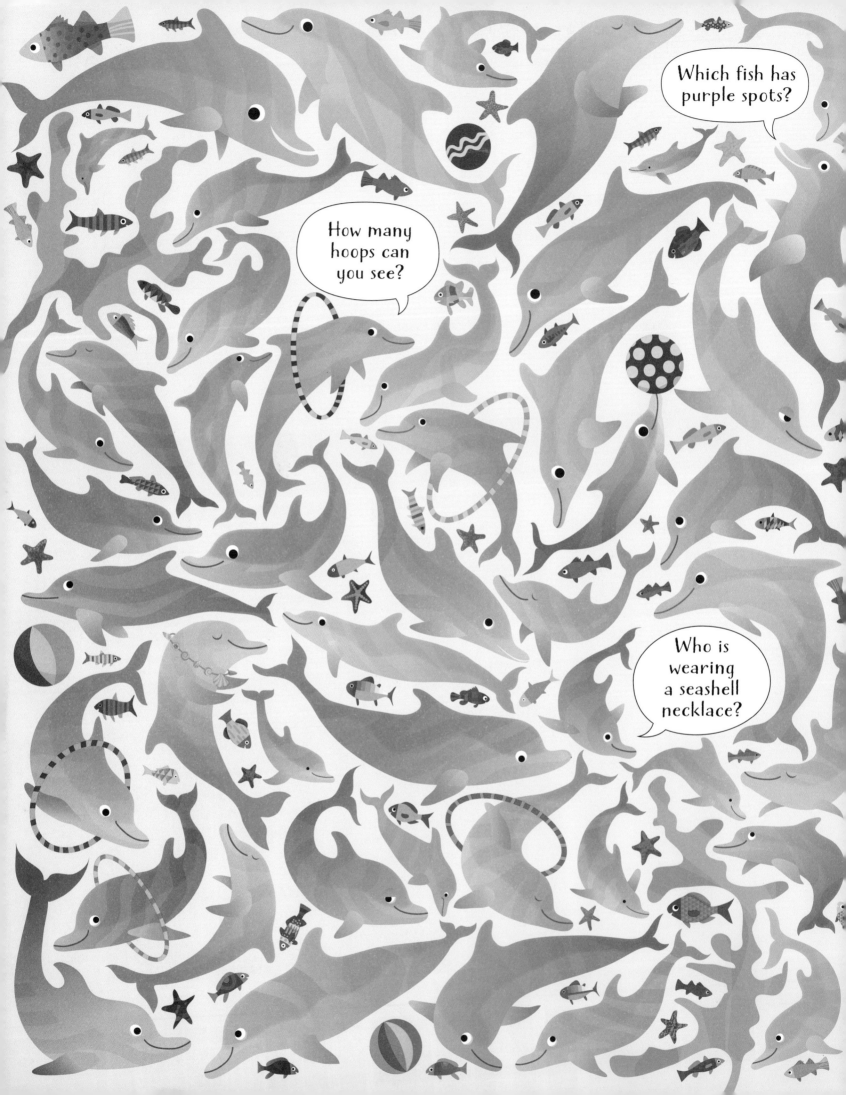

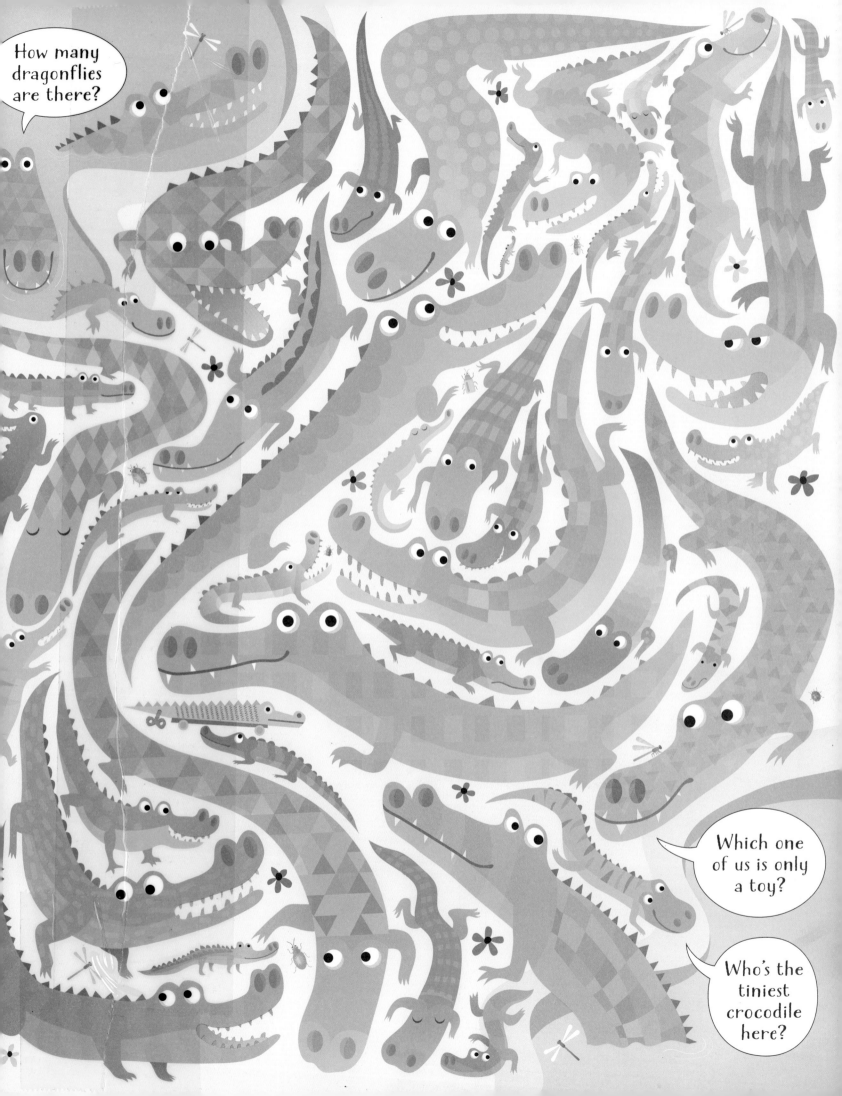

16

21

Where's the lunch box a visitor left behind?

Spot a guinea pig in a wig.

Can you see my penguin friend?

29

ANSWERS

Cover

2–3

4–5

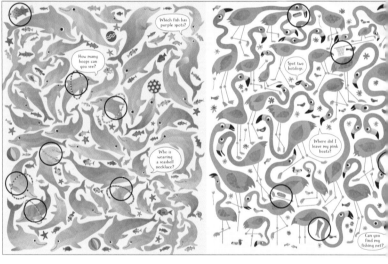

6–7

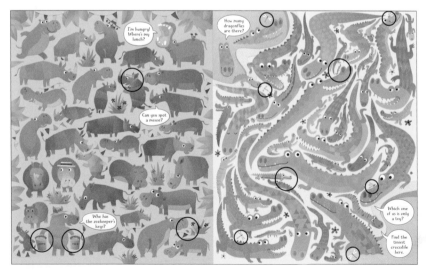

8–9

10–11

30

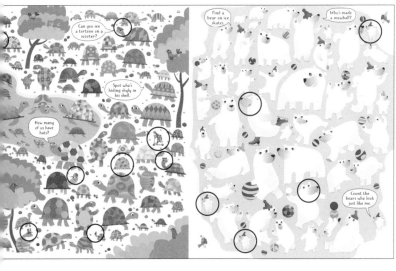

12-13

14-15

16-17

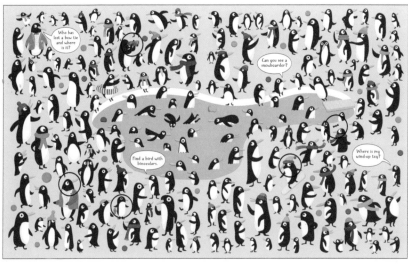

18-19

20-21

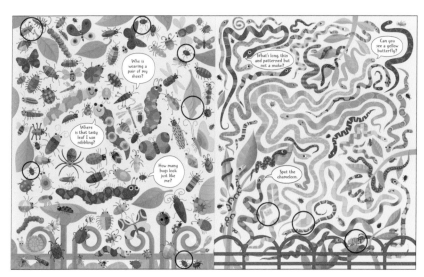

22-23

ANSWERS (continued)

24-25

26-27

28-29

This edition first published in 2017 by Usborne Publishing Ltd., Usborne House, 83–85 Saffron Hill, London, EC1N 8RT, England. www.usborne.com
Copyright © 2017, 2015 Usborne Publishing Ltd. The name Usborne and the devices ♀ ☺ are Trade Marks of Usborne Publishing Ltd. All rights reserved.
No part of this publication may be reproduced, stored in a retrieval system, or transmitted in any form or by any means, electronic, mechanical,
photocopying, recording or otherwise, without the prior permission of the publisher. UE. Printed in China.